Wilderness Meditations

40 Devotions for Lent, Fasting, and Spiritual Growth

Donna E. Lane, Ph.D.

ISBN-13: 978-1534666023

ISBN-10: 1534666028

Table of Contents

Acknowledgements

I would like to thank my husband, Dr. David Lane, for his patience and support throughout this process – for the extremely early alarms, which woke you, even though this Lenten "sacrifice" was meant for me and not for you; for the endless questions and requests for feedback; for the two hundred times I asked *again* if you understood, liked, got something out of, and thought other people would understand my writing; for your encouragement, checking in with how it was going and making sure I stayed with it; for the sacrifice of silent Thursdays, when I was editing and rewriting and adding to the original with my face embedded in the computer and my responses to you nonexistent; for tolerating music when you preferred quiet; and, for putting up with my hard-headedness. Most of all, thank you for loving me through the years, no matter what the circumstances.

I would also like to thank Andrea Newell, for her support, guidance, and friendship – for our weekly lunch discussions, exploring deep concepts about our relationships with God; for being open and willing to share your heart with me, trusting me to handle it with care; for offering freely those things which Jesus shared with you; and for praying with me and for me over these many years.

I would also like to thank my children, now grown: Hayden Lane and Dr. Lindsey Lane Verlander. Thank you for your love and support, for trusting me with your hearts, and for making the transition from parent-children to adult friends so smoothly. Thank you, Hayden, for sharing your brilliant ideas and insights, and for being willing to debate me and challenge me to deeper thinking and understanding. Thank you, Lindsey, for showing me a beautiful example of a life lived freely and teaching me how to more fully express joy. I love you both more than words can express!

Finally, I would like to thank my son, Cody – for his unsurpassed example of what it means to live life in the Kingdom of God in the here and now. I miss the warmth of your touch, but carry in my heart the warmth of your spirit.

Dedication

For Cody

Who touched as many lives as he could before he went home,

and who continues to touch lives –

I am looking forward to the end of the interim

All Biblical references are from the New International Version (NIV).

NIV Archaeological Study Bible: An Illustrated Walk through Biblical History and Culture. Grand Rapids, MI: Zondervan, 2005.

For additional information, books, and resources, go to:

DonnaandDavidLane.com

RestoredChristianity.com

CodyLaneFoundation.com

Like us on Facebook:

Facebook.com/Restored.Christianity

Facebook.com/codylanefoundation

Introduction

This book of daily meditations grew out of a request from the Lord. He asked of me that, instead of "giving up" something for Lent, I would arise earlier than normal each day, pray to ask for direction and focus, and write each day based on what I was hearing from the Lord in prayer. As a result, each daily meditation focuses on a different subject or theme, but hopefully as a whole the devotions present an interrelated and comprehensive view of our partnership with Christ. For each day, the theme for that day's meditation is identified at the end of the writing.

Lent begins on Ash Wednesday, and ends at Easter. Although there are 46 days between Ash Wednesday and Easter Sunday, Lent excludes the six Sundays between those two days, so when using this book of meditations, you will not have a specific writing for any of the Sundays until you get to Palm Sunday and Easter. I recommend using Sunday as a day of silence and worship, where you simply sit with Jesus and allow Him to speak to you and to show you His deep love for you. I enjoy closing my eyes and, like a little child with a loving Father, crawling up in His lap to be held in His arms. However, if it helps you to have something to talk with Jesus about in order to make that connection, you could review the previous week's themes and ask Him to speak on those themes as a whole.

I recommend that you read the meditation each morning while in prayer, asking Jesus to reveal to you His thoughts in order to expand on what is written and to focus on specific areas that will benefit you the most. After reading the meditation, I would suggest sitting quietly to listen for the Lord's response and engagement with you about the writing. I would urge setting aside a minimum of 15 minutes but as much time as you can focus effectively for reading, contemplating, and prayer for each day.

I also recommend that you choose music that is meaningful to you to listen to as you meditate. Music activates a different part of your brain than language, so listening to music engages more of your brain in the meditation process, which can be very beneficial. You can choose Christian contemporary music, Christian praise and worship, hymns, instrumental, classical, or any other form of music that helps you to feel at peace and to settle into a prayerful attitude for meditation. However, if you choose songs with lyrics such as Christian contemporary music, seek songs whose themes match the theme of the daily writing whenever that is possible. For example, the Ash Wednesday theme for meditation is "He is worthy." There are many songs whose lyrics focus on Jesus' worthiness, so choose one that speaks to your heart on this theme. Remember, peace and calm is the goal, so stay away from loud and fast music with a heavy beat, as these types of songs will produce a different result physiologically than you are seeking with these meditations. Sometimes, movement such as stretching, yoga, or slow and rhythmic movement to music aids in focus and in listening as you meditate, so you may want to begin your morning prayer in a space that allows for movement as well as solitude. If you meditate more easily when still and silent, choose to follow those spiritual disciplines instead of using music and movement.

Once you have completed the 40 days of meditations, I encourage you to go back through them and highlight themes or areas that touched your heart in a special and meaningful way. Reread the associated Scriptures, including all of the verses surrounding the ones that are included in these writings, and as the Lord leads, complete some additional study on those themes and verses. The writings are intentionally brief in order to best facilitate following through on meditating daily; however, for those themes of significance to you, more study and exploration would be valuable.

Even though the meditations were originally written for Lent, and the daily titles may correspond to specific days during the lead up to the Passion of Christ, the writings are also appropriate for other uses, such as a 40-day fast or a retreat focused on building a closer relationship with Jesus. It isn't necessary that you restrict your use of these meditations to a specific time or for a specific purpose. I encourage you to follow the Lord's lead on how you can most benefit from the truths He has shared in these meditations.

The goal of this book is to help you reach a heart-level connection with Jesus daily, and through that connection to gain a deeper understanding of who Jesus is as well as to begin to establish a continuous communication with Christ as your norm throughout the day. I believe that prayer is a two-way communication, and that in fact the bulk of prayer needs to be focused on listening to what Jesus has to say. It is my hope that Jesus can use these simple writings as a starting point for opening up that ongoing, two-way communication with you, by giving you a focal topic to begin asking Him for revelation and truth. I anticipate that, after the 40 days of meditations are completed, you will realize that Jesus is present with you and desires to talk with you all day, at all times, about everything in your life. I pray that this type of communication with the Lord will endure for the rest of your life.

Ash Wednesday

Lent is intended to mirror Jesus' forty days in the wilderness, where He prepared His heart for His ultimate purpose through fasting and solitude. After fasting, He was tempted by Satan to abandon His purpose in exchange for self-gratification, self-acknowledgement, and power and control (Matthew 4:1-11). Jesus responded to the taunting of the enemy by using the truth of God, which serves as an example for us of what to do in the face of temptations that we, too, face daily. Just like Jesus prepared for His mission, the purpose of Lent is to prepare our hearts through self-sacrifice, self-denial, and prayer, as well as opening our hearts through repentance.

To begin the preparation of our hearts, I want us to contemplate the story of Christ, and see through His story what we can learn about Who He is. We know He left the throne of heaven and placed Himself willingly as an infant in the care of a teenage girl and a young man who chose to trust God in spite of the apparent circumstances. We know that, even though He was in His nature God, He "did not consider equality with God something to be used to his own advantage; rather, he made himself nothing by taking the very nature of a servant, being made in human likeness" (Philippians 2:6-7). We know He turned the practice of the Law upside down and restored it to its heart, even while He set out to fulfill the Law in its entirety (Matthew 5-7). We know that He "demonstrates his own love for us in this: while we were still sinners, Christ died for us" (Romans 5:8).

Of greatest importance, we know "that Christ died for our sins according to the Scriptures, that he was buried, that he was raised on the third day according to the Scriptures" (I Corinthians 15:3-4), for this is the gospel and the foundation of all that we believe. And we know that God found Jesus' sacrifice worthy to pay for our sin in total, to cancel the debt of death against us, and to restore us back to our original connection with God. As we consider

Jesus' story, let's fill our hearts to overflowing with the same conclusion as the angels in heaven, so that we always remember, "Worthy is the Lamb, who was slain, to receive power and wealth and wisdom and strength and honor and glory and praise!" (Revelation 5:12).

Ash Wednesday reminds us, "for dust you are and to dust you will return" (Genesis 3:18), but because of Christ, we are "beauty instead of ashes" (Isaiah 61:3). The theme for meditation today is HE IS WORTHY.

Notes

Day Two

For the second day of Lent, I want to focus on how the Lord carries me – all of my weakness, my sin, my grief, my brokenness, my need, my whole heart. One of my favorite verses is Psalm 121:1-2 "I lift up my eyes to the mountains—where does my help come from? My help comes from the LORD, the Maker of heaven and earth." When my youngest son, Cody, died at age 17 from a degenerative neurological disorder, I literally could not stand. I described it to my friends as feeling like I had been flattened against the earth with an unimaginable and unbearable weight. My heart felt like it had fallen into a black hole, and all of my spirit had been sucked in behind it, leaving a vacuum-like void in my inner being. My grief felt like a part of myself had died with Cody. "But you, God, see the trouble of the afflicted; you consider their grief and take it in hand." (Psalm 10:14). Throughout those first months, Psalm 121 expressed the ache of my heart and the cry of my soul. I know Who carried me through each moment. I know Whose strength it was that got me out of bed, and Whose love comforted me at night. I finally understood the verse, "Blessed are those who mourn, for they will be comforted" (Matthew 5:4). The blessing of mourning is that Jesus is there to comfort you in the midst of it.

While Jesus carried me and comforted me, He also brought me truth that helped my heart. His gentleness with my hurting heart gradually prepared the way for understanding the vast redemption of Cody's life that God had provided. He was also able to show me, both through what Cody shared with us before he died and through Jesus' own revelation, how Cody was experiencing his life in the Kingdom. I was encouraged to know that I would soon see Cody again, fully restored as God created Him to be before illness ravaged his body, and as Cody said before he went home, "it is only an interim."

"God is our refuge and strength, an ever-present help in trouble. Therefore we will not fear, though the earth give way and the mountains fall into the heart of the sea, though its waters roar and foam and the mountains quake with their surging…the Lord Almighty is with us." (Psalm 46:1-3, 7). The theme for meditation today is HE IS MY HELP.

Notes

Day Three

For the third day of Lent, I want to focus on His work that was completed on the cross. Please consider the weight of this statement: the payment for all sin has been completely and totally made. My sin has been obliterated. Finished. Done for. Eradicated. Kaput. Nada. Gone. This is the Good News! The gift of God is freely given and fulfilled; all that is left for me to choose is if I am going to receive the gift. When Jesus looks at me, He sees someone made holy and pure by His sacrifice. He sees me as He created me, and if I look through His eyes, I can see myself the way He sees me. Any other view of sin diminishes the work of the cross and demeans the blood spilled by Christ. Since Jesus has made the payment for me in full, I don't want to return power to sin by focusing on it or giving in to it or judging and shaming myself for it. As Paul states, "For sin shall no longer be your master, because you are not under the law, but under grace." (Romans 6:14).

While the wages of sin is certainly death, the cross has paid the debt in full and the blood of Jesus has covered me completely. Yes, I am cleansed. That doesn't mean sin has no consequences. Consequences are not the same things as the debt owed from sin. In fact, out of love for us, the consequences of sin have been built into the design of the world, so that I will learn and not continue in the sin. If we did not have consequence of pain on our hand from putting our hand on a stove, we would keep putting our hand there until we completely destroyed our hand. The pain tells us there is something wrong and instructs us not to keep doing what we are doing. However, because of the cross of Christ, I no longer seek to avoid sin due to the payment due from sin (the fear of death), but hopefully I have grown up to the desire to not sin out of love for Christ instead of out of fear of condemnation. So, "thanks be to God that, though you used to be slaves to sin, you have come to obey from your heart the pattern of teaching that has now claimed your allegiance. You have been set free from sin and have become slaves to righteousness." (Romans 6:17-18).

"He has washed me clean, and I have been made whiter than snow" (Psalm 51:7). The theme for meditation today is HE MADE ME CLEAN.

Notes

Day Four

For the fourth day of Lent, I want to focus on His presence in our hearts. What an astounding truth: that God of the heavens and earth, the Maker of the universe, would choose to live within us! The boundless nature of His love for us is made evident in that choice. Jesus makes His desire clear: that we would remain in Him, as He remains in us (John 15:4). Countless times He calls us to His arms, to rest with Him, to abide in Him, to be sheltered under His wing, to be upheld by His hand, and to dwell in Him. His truth demonstrates His closeness and our security in His hands. Here are just a few of those many verses: Psalm 3:3; Psalm 4:8; Psalm 16:8; Psalm 18:2 and 35; Psalm 27:5; Psalm 28:7; Psalm 32:7; Psalm 61:4; Psalm 62:1 and 5; Psalm 63:8; Psalm 73:23; Psalm 84; Psalm 91:1; Psalm 119:114; Psalm 139:1-18; Isaiah 28:12-13; Isaiah 30:15; Isaiah 32:17-18; Isaiah 41:13; Ezekiel 37:26-27; Hosea 14:7; Matthew 11:28-29; Acts 2:25-26; I Corinthians 3:16; Ephesians 3:16-18; Hebrews 4:1-10; Revelation 21:3.

From these verses we learn that God, rather than being an observer of our lives, is our partner. He longs to shelter us in His arms and uphold us by His hand. He is a very present and willing participant. He guards us with truth and love. He walks before us like a shield, taking the blows meant for us, because whatever comes toward us that does not match His truth does not get through if we keep our eyes on Him. He stands behind us like a guard who has our back, with watchful care over each step we take, because His warning in our spirits keeps us from being blindsided if we listen only to His voice. He strides beside us like a guide, leading and helping but never demanding or controlling, and never enabling us by doing it for us or pitying us as victims. He remains over us like a covering, and below us blocking hell's attacks. In other words, He surrounds us as our hiding place and fortress.

"Remain in me, as I also remain in you. No branch can bear fruit by itself; it must remain in the vine. Neither can you bear fruit unless you remain in me. I am the vine; you are the branches. If you remain in me and I in you, you will bear much fruit; apart from me you can do nothing." (John 15:4-5). My partner has made the way for me to be with Him, and He has chosen to live in me. The theme for meditation today is HE LIVES IN ME.

Notes

Day Five

For Day Five of Lent, I thought I would focus on one of Cody's most cherished beliefs: that we can listen for the voice of Jesus and He will tell us the truth we need to be truly free. Some contend that God spoke everything He had to say in the Bible; however, the Bible itself would disagree with this assertion. Jeremiah 31:33 says, "This is the covenant I will make with the people of Israel after that time," declares the LORD. "I will put my law in their minds and write it on their hearts. I will be their God, and they will be my people." In John 16:12-14, Jesus states, "I have much more to say to you, more than you can now bear. But when he, the Spirit of truth, comes, he will guide you into all the truth. He will not speak on his own; he will speak only what he hears, and he will tell you what is yet to come. He will glorify me because it is from me that he will receive what he will make known to you." II Corinthians 13:14 says, "May the grace of the Lord Jesus Christ, and the love of God, and the fellowship of the Holy Spirit be with you all," indicating Paul's desire that the believers to whom he was writing would experience the ongoing presence and relationship with Jesus through the Holy Spirit that he experienced. Thus, we have indications in the Old Testament, the gospels, and the letters of Paul that God still speaks to our hearts.

These verses are just a few examples of many verses that state clearly that God continues to interact and relate to His people. Once I accept that hearing Jesus speak to me in my heart is possible, I will open my heart and mind to the manner in which He desires to speak to me. Each individual is unique, so the way He speaks to you may not be the same as the manner in which He speaks to me. The one commonality is that what He speaks to us all is Truth, and His truth brings us freedom.

"You will know the truth, and the truth will set you free." (John 8:32) The theme for meditation today is HE IS THE TRUTH.

Notes

Day Six

For Day Six of Lent, I want to focus on God's mighty power. As Lent aptly points out, we are nothing but dust, save for the mighty power of Jesus Christ to overcome death and to free us from the consequences of our sin by taking those consequences on Himself. Because of His mighty power, we will live on, not just in the memories of others, not because of something we have accomplished, but in eternal reality. And He has given us access to His mighty power in this present age: the power to overcome the lies of the enemy with truth, the power to stand up and express our true nature, the power to show His incomparable love to others. As Paul writes, "his incomparably great power for us who believe…is the same as the mighty strength he exerted when he raised Christ from the dead and seated him at his right hand in the heavenly realms, far above all rule and authority, power and dominion, and every name that is invoked, not only in the present age but also in the one to come." (Ephesians 1:19-21).

Because Jesus lives in us, we have access to His mighty power. II Corinthians 4:7 is clear that we have all-surpassing power, and that this power is from God. Therefore: "We are hard pressed on every side, but not crushed; perplexed, but not in despair; persecuted, but not abandoned; struck down, but not destroyed." (II Corinthians 4:8-9). It is God Who provides for the continuation and perseverance of our spirit. Everything that matters and all of our needs are provided by God. "Therefore we do not lose heart. Though outwardly we are wasting away, yet inwardly we are being renewed day by day. For our light and momentary troubles are achieving for us an eternal glory that far outweighs them all." (II Corinthians 4:16-17).

In my heart, His power moves me and strengthens me to fight the battle, while He renews my spirit with His love and truth: "those who hope in the LORD will renew their strength.
They will soar on wings like eagles; they will run and not grow

weary, they will walk and not be faint." (Isaiah 40:31). The theme for meditation today is HE IS MIGHTY.

Notes

Day Seven

For Day Seven of Lent, I want to focus on the safety and peace of resting in God's arms. We easily get worried and fretful and overwhelmed and busy with the things of this world when our eyes are focused on ourselves and the world's perspectives. But when we rest in God's presence, all of those things simply fade into the background, and if we then choose to follow His lead, He will be a refuge through any difficulty and protect us within the fortress of His truth, so that our lives can be filled with genuine peace. "Whoever dwells in the shelter of the Most High will rest in the shadow of the Almighty. I will say of the LORD, "He is my refuge and my fortress, my God, in whom I trust." (Psalm 91:1-2).

Satan seeks to turn our eyes from the truth of God's rest and onto the chaos of the world. We want God to prevent difficulties, but that is the one thing that is not promised. In fact, we are told we will have trouble in this world (John 16:33), and we will suffer many things due to evil's efforts against us; however, we are promised His rest as well. Circumstances come and go; situations wax and wane. Our security and stability is in His abiding presence with us, no matter what comes.

Why is it important to God that we rest? What is the significance of solitude and quiet with Jesus? Rest is directly opposite to a devaluing of ourselves, because resting in Him meets both our needs and our desires. Rest provides restoration, recovery, and replenishing of our spirit and our joy. Rest returns us to God. Satan uses a lack of rest, through busyness and demanding of us to systematically pull us away from God, to wear us down, and to ultimately cover up who we truly are. The enemy's desire is that we are left as if we are in a desert without water. Jesus, however, is clear that He is our living water, and that whoever receives His water will never thirst. As He stated, "Indeed, the water I give them will become in them a spring of water welling up to eternal life." (John 4:14).

So, take His yoke upon you (instead of the burdens and busyness and demands of the world) and learn from Him, for He is gentle and humble in heart, and you will find rest for your souls. (Matthew 11:29). The theme for meditation today is HE IS MY REST.

Notes

Day Eight

For Day Eight of Lent, I want to focus on the joy of the Lord. We are told that the joy of the Lord is our strength (Nehemiah 8:10) – so no wonder we often live our lives in a kind of weak and dismal survival mode, with our heads down, looking ahead to some future day for hope: we have no joy! Then where does joy come from? Certainly, we know it does not come from worldly things for no wealth or accomplishment or status or substance can give us real, deep, and lasting joy. As Jesus taught, "Do not store up for yourselves treasures on earth, where moths and vermin destroy, and where thieves break in and steal. But store up for yourselves treasures in heaven, where moths and vermin do not destroy, and where thieves do not break in and steal. For where your treasure is, there your heart will be also." (Matthew 6:19-21).

Joy is found in trusting Him with your heart and relying on His presence. Joy is found in sharing experiences with Him, so that your eyes are opened to the wonder, beauty, and life-giving sustenance of His creation. Joy is found in feeling the indescribable love He feels when He gazes at you, knowing that He truly sees you for who you are and knows your heart like no one else can. Joy is found in being free to completely express who you are created to be, because He is the One Who created you that way. Joy is finding the treasure of the Kingdom hidden in a field, going and selling everything you have in order to buy the field and gain the treasure (Matthew 13:44). Joy is found in praising and worshipping, allowing your heart to overflow with love for Jesus, because you know Who He is and what He has done for you. Joy is fully grasping "how wide and long and high and deep is the love of Christ, and to know this love that surpasses knowledge" (Ephesians 3:18-19), and joy is being "filled to the measure of all the fullness of God." (Ephesians 3:19).

"The LORD is my strength and my shield; my heart trusts in him, and he helps me. My heart leaps for joy, and with my song I praise him."

(Psalm 28:7). The theme for meditation today is HE IS MY STRENGTH.

Notes

Day Nine

For Day Nine of Lent, I want to focus on what it means to have faith. The story of Peter stepping out of the boat to walk to the outstretched and calling arms of the Lord is a picture of what it means to have faith, and Peter sinking helps us to understand why faith collapses and what happens when it does (Matthew 14:28-32). Amazingly, it was at Peter's suggestion that Jesus called Him to come out onto the water. All Peter saw as he stood on the edge of the boat ready to walk out was Jesus. As he stepped onto the water, Peter's eyes were glued onto Him alone. It wasn't until Peter started noticing the wind and the waves, taking his eyes off of the Lord, that he began to sink.

Faith isn't magical thinking or trying to make ourselves believe in something. Faith isn't crossing our fingers and hoping fate will smile on us, or luck will lean our way. Faith isn't believing things will turn out like we want it to, or circumstances will go our way. According to Hebrews 11:1, faith is knowing that when God says something, it is, whether we see it or not (because we have our eyes on Him), and faith is being certain of the Lord. Faith is being persuaded (the actual meaning of the Greek word for faith) in our belief (in other words, convinced – certain – confident – sure). The essence of faith is answered in where we focus our eyes. Just like Peter, if we fix our eyes on Jesus, we will see through His eyes, and understand based on His truth. If we turn our eyes to ourselves or to the world for answers and understanding, we will sink.

"So we fix our eyes not on what is seen, but on what is unseen, since what is seen is temporary, but what is unseen is eternal." (II Corinthians 4:18). The theme for meditation today is HE CALLS ME OUT.

Notes

Day Ten

For Day Ten of Lent, I want to focus on the name of Jesus. When I wake in the morning, His is the first name that I speak. When I have a question, His is the name that I reach out to. When I am in trouble or in pain, His is the name that I call on. When I have needs or desires of my heart, His is the name that I lean on. Someone who does not know Him would think this foolishness; "For the message of the cross is foolishness to those who are perishing, but to us who are being saved it is the power of God." (I Corinthians 1:18). What is the importance of the name of Jesus?

We call on His name because naming gives reality to identity. In both the Old and New Testament, names signified the nature and identity of the individual or place. Abraham and his descendants named locations based on the significance and meaning of the events that happened at that place. Jacob's name reflected his nature. Jesus renamed Simon Peter to signify his significance as the rock on which the church is built. Saul was renamed Paul to indicate he had been made new by Christ, and as a result he had a new identity. So praying and calling on the name of Jesus means I am communicating with Him under His identity. In other words, if we don't know Him, we don't know who He is, and if we don't know who He is we don't relate to Him or connect with Him. If we don't connect we cannot communicate, and don't hear His voice.

There is power in the name of Jesus. Scripture tells us that by the name of Jesus, people are healed (Acts 3:16, 4:10), that demons are commanded and must obey (Acts 16:18), and that we are sanctified and justified (I Corinthians 6:11). "God exalted him to the highest place and gave him the name that is above every name, that at the name of Jesus every knee should bow, in heaven and on earth and under the earth, and every tongue acknowledge that Jesus Christ is Lord, to the glory of God the Father." (Philippians 2:9-11). That is true power.

Because I know Him, my heart cries out Jesus,
"For to me, to live is Christ and to die is gain." (Philippians 1:21).
The theme for meditation today is HE IS THE NAME ABOVE ALL NAMES.

Notes

Day Eleven

For Day Eleven of Lent, I want to focus on the water of life. We took a boat out on the lake recently, and as we were speeding over the water, wind in our faces and surrounded by nature's beauty, I felt Jesus' enjoyment as He shared in the experience with me. So I said to Him, "You really enjoy the water, don't You?" He responded, "Water is life."

I was immediately struck by the amazing way God has reflected truth within the very nature of His creation. As Paul explains, "For since the creation of the world God's invisible qualities—his eternal power and divine nature—have been clearly seen, being understood from what has been made, so that people are without excuse." (Romans 1:20). Physically, it is a truth that water is life. We cannot survive without it. Our most important organs – our brain and heart (mind and soul) – are over 70% water, and our lungs (breath of life) are over 80% water. Jesus said, "whoever drinks the water I give them will never thirst. Indeed, the water I give them will become in them a spring of water welling up to eternal life" (John 4:14). The truth of our need for Christ's free gift of "living water" is reflected in our very bodies, and experienced fully in our spirits.

All of us know what it means to be thirsty. Thirst is our body expressing need, and physically, we need water more than we need anything else. We can survive without food for 40 days or more but without water we will die in as few as 3 days. Every single cell in our body needs it. So when Jesus talked about drinking the living water He gives us to never thirst again, He was giving us a clear picture of our unparalleled need for Him for our very lives. We cannot live without Him.

"If you knew the gift of God…, you would have asked him and he would have given you living water." (John 4:10). The theme for meditation today is HE IS LIVING WATER.

Notes

Day Twelve

For Day Twelve of Lent, I want to focus on our home. As it stands, we are aliens in a foreign land, separated from our true realm like the Israelites were when they lived in Babylon during their captivity. And like Israel, we must learn how to live as foreigners, keeping to our own beliefs and convictions and following our God in the face of multiple "local gods," such as wealth, power, superiority, pride, and possession. These are our "Nebuchadnezzar," and we must not bow to these foreign gods. This is not where we belong. "If you belonged to the world, it would love you as its own. As it is, you do not belong to the world, but I have chosen you out of the world." (John 15:19).

Our true home is with God. For us right now, His Kingdom is where He is with us, which is in our hearts. Jesus explained this truth to His disciples: "I will ask the Father, and he will give you another advocate to help you and be with you forever— the Spirit of truth. The world cannot accept him, because it neither sees him nor knows him. But you know him, for he lives with you and will be in you. I will not leave you as orphans; I will come to you. Before long, the world will not see me anymore, but you will see me. Because I live, you also will live. On that day you will realize that I am in my Father, and you are in me, and I am in you." (John 14:16-20). Because of this truth, we know the Kingdom of God is with us now, for it is within us.

However, soon, we will go home once more, and His Kingdom will surround us. He has prepared this place for us, as He said He would. "My Father's house has many rooms; if that were not so, would I have told you that I am going there to prepare a place for you? And if I go and prepare a place for you, I will come back and take you to be with me that you also may be where I am." (John 14:2-3). The theme for meditation today is HE IS MY HOME.

Notes

Day Thirteen

For Day Thirteen of Lent, I want to talk about our focus. When training for childbirth, women are taught to find a "focal point" and to fix on that focal point during each contraction. This focus diminishes the pain because everything other than the focal point fades into the background. The birthing mother is not giving attention to anything else. Basically, everything else dims except the one thing we are fully focused on. Thus, it matters what we choose to focus on in our lives, because what we focus on will consume our thoughts, our attention, our emotions, and our reality.

The enemy likes to pull our attention onto things that don't matter by convincing us that they are important, that we are entitled to them, that we need them or want them, and even that we will not be happy without them. Satan offers us brightly wrapped candy, very appealing to the eye and enticing in what he purports that it provides us. If we take it and eat it, we will taste sweetness - but just for a moment. The candy then turns bitter in our mouths and the bitterness is so awful, we become desperate for something to take that bitter taste away. Of course, Satan offers another piece of candy and the sweetness brings what feels to us like relief - for a moment. Our desperation grows as the bitterness deepens, and we start seeking his candy on our own because we think anything is better than the bitter taste. We are blinded to the fact that it was Satan's candy that produced the bitterness in the first place. As Scripture warns us, "Though evil is sweet in his mouth and he hides it under his tongue, though he cannot bear to let it go and keeps it in his mouth, yet his food will turn sour in his stomach, it will become the venom of serpents within him" (Job 20:12-14).

Scripture tells us where to focus our eyes: "my eyes are fixed on you, Sovereign LORD; in you I take refuge" (Psalm 141:8); "fixing our eyes on Jesus, the pioneer and perfecter of faith." (Hebrews 12:2). What flows from that choice is everything worldly fades, and our consuming reality is Jesus and the ways of His Kingdom. The theme for meditation today is HE IS MY FOCUS.

Notes

Day Fourteen

For Day Fourteen of Lent, I want to talk about God's grace. His grace is seen in every kindness and every act of love. It is reflected in the beauty of every sunrise and the glory of every sunset, and in the magnificence of each mountain peak and ocean wave. It carries us during our deepest losses, and helps us through our most difficult struggles. Whatever is good and pure in this life comes from His grace.

Paul stood on the truth that only the grace of God can save us, and the cross is sufficient. This is such a critical underpinning that Paul talks about being "cut in on" in the race by any other belief. (Galatians 5:7). Our salvation is only by the blood of Christ through the grace of God, righteousness only comes through the Spirit, and the only thing that counts is faith expressing itself through love. "You who are trying to be justified by the law have been alienated from Christ; you have fallen away from grace." (Galatians 5:4). This is no small thing Paul is saying – we cannot hedge our bets; we cannot have it both ways. The sin nature is at war with the Spirit. I want to be the god of my own life, and this temptation is repeatedly presented to us just like in Eden. Adam and Eve's temptation is the same deception we face each day. Will I eat the fruit and try to create my own salvation by pursuing my own justification? We are easily swayed by our sin nature to cling to our self-justification through our actions, and along the same lines, we are quick to condemn ourselves for falling short in our actions, as if those mistakes can undo the cross and remove us from grace. No! According to Paul, binding ourselves to the law alienates us from Christ and pulls us away from the loving arms of His grace. Paul goes on to say that the entire law is summed up in love, and that we are to live by the Spirit. In other words, we are not on our own; love and the Spirit are to direct our path. This truth is the grace of God.

But the most amazing thing about His grace is it is freely given, and nothing we can do or say can earn it or change it. We live by His grace. "For it is by grace you have been saved, through faith—and this is not from yourselves, it is the gift of God" (Ephesians 2:8). The theme for meditation today is HE IS GRACE.

Notes

Day Fifteen

For Day Fifteen of Lent, I want to talk about the battle. Sometimes we get complacent because we look around us and think, "What battle?" But if we see with spiritual eyes, we will see that not only are we part of an ongoing war, but beyond that, we are soldiers behind enemy lines. This is the most dangerous, the most at-risk, and the most exposed position of any soldier, and it is the position that requires the most discipline and skill. When difficult circumstances and suffering happen to us, we are getting a taste of the reality of the battle we are in; however, the battle doesn't cease when the difficulty passes, and we need to understand how vital it is that we keep fighting wisely and persistently, using the implements of war that we have been given and responding strategically to the tactics of the enemy.

Every thought that comes into our minds is someone knocking at the door of our inner "house." Just like we would do in our earthly home, we need to check and see who it is before we open the door wide and let just anyone come in for dinner at our table. When a thought comes, stop and look to see the source of that thought – is it Jesus or is it the enemy of God? This process is the fundamental meaning of "take every thought captive" (II Corinthians 10:5). Unfortunately, we tend to open our door wide for every thought without consideration. We take ownership of any and every thought as our own, rather than recognizing the source, and in doing so, we let all thoughts enter, whether for good or for evil, whether for benefit or for destruction. In owning all thoughts, and not considering the source before we accept them, we make the enemy's job much easier than it needs to be. Imagine what it would be like if every robber, thief, or murderer found your door wide open to them and discovered you sleeping, without defense. That is how most of us live our spiritual lives, without any awareness that we are doing something we would never do in the earthly realm. It is time to take God's admonition to war seriously!

Mainly, we need to remember who fights by our side on our behalf, and call on Jesus for truth, for training, for leadership and direction, and for help in the struggle. "Finally, be strong in the Lord and in his mighty power. Put on the full armor of God, so that you can take your stand against the devil's schemes." (Ephesians 6:10-11). The theme for meditation today is HE HEARS MY CRY.

Notes

Day Sixteen

For Day Sixteen of Lent, I want to talk about being God's child. No matter what anyone says about me; no matter what has happened to me in my life; no matter what Satan lies about me in my ear; no matter my circumstances or mistakes or sins – I am His child and He loves me with His whole being. I am fearfully and wonderfully made in His image (Psalm 139:14). Some aspect or aspects of His nature are reflected in me, as His child and heir. Whatever aspects of His nature He knit together within me (Psalm 139:13) are like a beautiful diamond, precious beyond price and more valuable than can be measured. The circumstances that happen to me in this sin-infused life, the sin-based choices I make, the opinions and attitudes of others toward me, and the beliefs that I form in my heart as a result of or response to those experiences, are like dirt that is cast onto my diamond. If enough dirt is thrown, it may eventually cover up the diamond completely, and I may lose sight of who I really am, as my nature as God's child and heir is hidden. However, dirt is not strong enough to alter or damage a diamond! From my creation and through all eternity, I am who God created me to be, and I reflect His facets in my heart.

With His help, I can uncover the diamond and allow it to shine with His light into the world around me. My circumstances have no power over me except the power I give them through beliefs that come from my interpretation of the circumstances; therefore, if God changes my beliefs to His truth, all the so-called power of those circumstances is removed. In the same way, the words spoken about me or to me have no power if I do not accept and believe them. On my own, I will succumb to the lies of the enemy, because those lies feel true to me, based on my perception of myself and my experiences. But if I ask Jesus to bring His truth to my heart, and I willingly listen and receive His truth, He can replace those lies, and my diamond can be restored.

Even if my earthly parents did not know me, love me, or recognize me as special, I have a Perfect Parent Who knows me, adores me, and protects me fiercely. "The Spirit you received brought about your adoption to sonship. And by him we cry, '*Abba,* Father.' The Spirit himself testifies with our spirit that we are God's children." (Romans 8:15-16). The theme for meditation today is HE IS MY TRUE FATHER.

Notes

Day Seventeen

For Day Seventeen of Lent, I want to focus on listening to God. His promise is that He would write His word on our hearts (Jeremiah 31:33); however, often we spend our prayer time talking to God and making requests of God instead of listening for His word for us. Christ Himself taught us that God speaks to us. Jesus promises His disciples He will not to leave them without help, and He goes on to state, "All this I have spoken while still with you. But the Advocate, the Holy Spirit, whom the Father will send in my name, will teach you all things and will remind you of everything I have said to you." (John 14:25-26). Again, Jesus told His disciples, "I have much more to say to you, more than you can now bear. But when he, the Spirit of truth, comes, he will guide you into all the truth. He will not speak on his own; he will speak only what he hears, and he will tell you what is yet to come." (John 16:12-13). His Spirit is promised to us, to teach us all things and to guide us into all truth. I would suggest that it is the presence of His Spirit living within us that makes it possible for us to receive and comprehend the truth – that it is His Spirit speaking to us that makes it possible for us to know truth in our hearts.

Jesus also promised us that we would be able to recognize His voice. He begins to explain this in John 10:3-5, where He teaches, "The gatekeeper opens the gate for him, and the sheep listen to his voice. He calls his own sheep by name and leads them out. When he has brought out all his own, he goes on ahead of them, and his sheep follow him because they know his voice. But they will never follow a stranger; in fact, they will run away from him because they do not recognize a stranger's voice." He goes on to say, "My sheep listen to my voice; I know them, and they follow me." (v. 27).

If we open our hearts and take the time in quiet to listen, He promises to respond. "Call to me and I will answer you and tell you great and unsearchable things you do not know." (Jeremiah 33:3). I want to encourage you to spend some significant time today with God, quietly listening, open to whatever He wants to say to you. The transformational power of God's truth spoken to our hearts cannot be described, it can only be experienced; but it is *promised*. Our part is to listen. The theme for meditation today is HE SPEAKS TO MY HEART.

Notes

Day Eighteen

For Day Eighteen of Lent, I want to focus on the never-ending love of God. From the beginning of Genesis through the end of Revelation, His story is the story of the loving pursuit of His children. His love for us has withstood our rejection, our denial, our abandonment, our betrayal, and our disdain, and it has never failed. In the face of all we have done, and all we didn't do, He still left the throne of heaven for our sakes, took the whip for our sakes, walked Calvary for our sakes, withstood the cross and its shame for our sakes, accepted death for our sakes, entered hell for our sakes, battled Satan for our sakes, and was resurrected for our sakes.

Satan obscures God's love by using the terminology of the truth but distorting its meaning and its heart, and losing its substance. Lacking the awakening of our hearts to the truth of God's love, we tend to see His love as permissiveness, or as a reason to feel guilty or the need to strive for approval. For example, some see the Law as an external standard, not a loving gift of God for our benefit. The standard of the Law is viewed as the measuring rod by which our value and worth is weighed, obscuring the LOVE behind the Law. A permissive, indulging parent is not a loving parent. A parent who said, "well, honey, if you want to go walk in the middle of the road, I don't want to restrict you or tell you 'no' so go ahead you're ok" would be guilty of child neglect. Limits for the child's protection are loving gifts from the parent. And that is what the Law is for us: not a standard by which we measure our value and acceptability to God, and not something that was only worth something to the Old Testament folks. As Paul said, the Law is a shadow of the good things that are coming, not the realities themselves (Hebrews 10:1) – in other words, the Law is a reflection of the love of God, made complete and fulfilled in the coming of Christ, and His death on the cross. If we externalize the Law and make it either nothing to us, or we make it the standard of our worth, we lose the reflection of the love of God in it. We miss the gift. If instead we grasp the love of God for us, we internalize the Law as our heart's desire. We receive and know that it is best for us, and we desire to do what is best because He desires it for us. Our love for God flows freely out of our hearts, coming from the love He has poured out into us, for our sakes.

He has done everything, even unto death, to love us. "Who shall separate us from the love of Christ? ….neither death nor life, neither angels nor demons, neither the present nor the future, nor any powers, neither height nor depth, nor anything else in all creation, will be able to separate us from the love of God that is in Christ Jesus our Lord." (Romans 8:36-39). The theme for meditation today is HIS LOVE NEVER FAILS.

Notes

Day Nineteen

For Day Nineteen of Lent, I want to talk about God creating our identity. Psalm 139:13 states, "For you created my inmost being; you knit me together in my mother's womb." It is the Artist – the Creator – Who knows more than anyone else about His work of art. You would not go to your plumber to get an accurate explanation of the symbolism and meaning in a poem, or to describe the story behind a painting. You would go to the source, the author of the poem or the painter of the artwork. In the same way, you would not trust anyone other than your Creator to tell you who you are. He sees us, from our first moment of being, as who we really are. What He does not see are the impositions of the enemy – the lie beliefs, the sins, and the woundings of this life – as He looks at His glorious child. He sees our true identity, and calls us who we are, naming us based not on what we have experienced, but based solely on the identity He created.

The identity of God and our identity as created by God and in relationship to God are the two foundational truths we all need to know. In the same way, then, it is important for us to know our "name" as given by God - our identity as He created us to be. The only way to truly know that is to first know Him, and then to ask Him who we are and what name He has given us.

Just as He named Peter based on who Peter really was, the rock, He names each of us anew. "I will also give that person a white stone with a new name written on it, known only to the one who receives it."(Revelation 2:17). In my case, He names me Helga Anna – His warrior who fights the enemy by His side, and His dancer who is fiercely and passionately in love with her partner. I encourage you to ask Jesus to give you your new name. The theme for meditation today is HE KNOWS MY NAME.

Notes

Day Twenty

For Day Twenty of Lent, I want to focus on God's redemption. So what does God as our Redeemer mean for us? First, of course, we know that He has saved us for eternal life with Him. This, in and of itself, is the most amazing, most glorious redemption. But His redemption isn't just a future promise, it is a present reality. So often, we miss His redemption because we aren't looking for it; we are focused instead on Satan's machinations or on our own interpretations and perceptions. But if Romans 8:28 is true, in saying "all things", then His redemption is present for us in all things. In order to truly understand the glory of His intervening redemption for us, we must begin with an understanding of where we are living: we are surrounded on all sides by enemy forces; evil consumes the air around us, presses hard against us, constantly taunts and tempts us, swirls in our thoughts and the thoughts of others, and unrelentingly seeks to steal, kill, and destroy us. If we truly understand this, then we know that, without the constant intervening hand of God, we would be reduced to nothing more than the worst of Sodom and Gomorrah. Except for the presence of God pursuing us, we would all be lost. If not for God fighting for us, we would all be destroyed. If God did not desire us and protect us, we would all be devoured. If left to our own devices, we would all become the essence of evil. So God's redemption helps us to become the people He created us to be instead of disappearing into Satan's evil mire and becoming a part of it.

On still another level, God takes those things that happen to us at the hands of the enemy, and through the power of His love, He turns them for good. The "good" can take many forms, and can be an immediate and/or a more long-term redemption, but it will come. For example, Cody was stricken with a sickness caused by a lie at 19 months of age, but God's redemption of Cody's life started that moment and continued through each and every day of his life. The amazing person Cody was and everything Cody accomplished was all produced through Cody's incredible relationship with Jesus. His life has had a tremendous impact on many, including his family, and he still impacts others even though he is home with his Jesus now. If we have the eyes to see God's redemption, how beautiful and loving a thing it is to behold.

Oftentimes, when we go through painful or traumatic events in our lives, we see those events as scarring us permanently. It might feel like what happened to us cannot be redeemed or we cannot recover, but Jesus, our Redeemer, overcomes, because truth is always stronger than any lie. His truth heals those wounds and breathes life back into us, replacing the enemy's lies and restoring us to wholeness, while He takes what Satan intended for evil and "works for the good of those who love Him" (Romans 8:28). The theme for meditation today is HE IS MY REDEEMER.

Notes

Day Twenty-one

For Day Twenty-one of Lent, I want to focus on Jesus as the main character in our life's story. He is the Hero Who rescues the damsel in distress from the clutches of the evil thief. He is the Wise Fatherly Man Who brings us wisdom and strength, who coaxes us into new understanding, and who leads us into truth. He is the Companion Who walks by our side as we navigate the difficult quest and Who carries us when we fall. He is the King Who establishes the order of the Kingdom and insures the safety of its people. He is the Warrior Who fights tirelessly on the front lines against invading forces and is victorious over the enemy. He is the Lover Who searches relentlessly for His bride and sweeps her off her feet to carry her off into the sunset. And most of all, He is God, Who dies in the place of the protagonist in the story.

Over and over again, we see the Lord reminding Israel of the story of God bringing them out of Egypt, and He instructs them to retell their story every year at Passover, so that every generation will remember their story, and thus remember their God. In the same way, Jesus instructed His disciples to associate the Passover story of Israel with His story, the story of the cross; and every time they celebrated with the bread and wine, they were to "do this in remembrance of Me." (Luke 22:19). Throughout Scripture we are told we must tell, and retell, the story in order to remember. I believe the same is true of our own stories with the Lord. It is important that others hear our story, in order to plant the seed for their own story of redemption to come to pass, and to encourage them with hope along the path of their journey. However, it is also important that we tell, and retell, our stories, so that *we* remember.

This may not be the story we would have imagined, but it is the story God told. Our story is an action-fantasy-epic quest-period piece-war saga-love story, the likes of which has never been seen before and will never be seen again. "Let the redeemed of the LORD tell their story— those he redeemed from the hand of the foe" (Psalm 107:2). The theme for mediation today is HE IS MY STORY.

Notes

Day Twenty-two

For Day Twenty-two of Lent, I want to focus on the light. I have always loved Isaiah 61: "He has sent me to bind up the brokenhearted…and release from darkness for the prisoners…to comfort all who mourn…to bestow on them a crown of beauty instead of ashes, the oil of joy instead of mourning, and a garment of praise instead of a spirit of despair." But these verses took on a whole new meaning for me when my son, Cody, died. That day, it felt like all light and life that had been in me had been consumed, and my heart had collapsed in on itself. It was darkness beyond darkness, like nothing I had ever experienced. At that point in my life, when light within me seemed to have gone away with Cody, I became a blind person, seemingly engulfed in total darkness. And when someone is blind, it doesn't matter if the light is on in the room and everyone else can see where they are going; the blind person does not know the light is on and cannot see their surroundings or how to navigate walking across the room.

Grief and loss are not the only kinds of darkness we experience. It is easy for our sin nature to gradually consume our light, by telling us that Jesus doesn't want us or we aren't good enough and cannot have Him, eventually leaving us blind and wandering in the dark. Shame is darkness in the form of a belief, as we cover our eyes and blind ourselves to avoid seeing and being seen. Fear also eradicates the light from our lives, sucking away all joy and tempting us to hide ourselves away in a dark cave for our supposed safety and protection from harm. Of course, the cave of our self-protection is actually a prison, and we become bound to the darkness, until we begin to believe we can never walk in the light again.

Jesus said, "I am the light of the world. Whoever follows me will never walk in darkness, but will have the light of life." (John 8:12). The light of Jesus – only Jesus – could reach into the darkness of my grief and find me. As He gently held me and loved me in my deep mourning, He gave me the blessing of His comfort and began to release me from the darkness. He tenderly restored my destroyed heart, and gave me back the joy of my memories with Cody to replace the ashes of my emptiness. The theme for meditation today is HE IS MY LIGHT.

Notes

Day Twenty-three

For Day Twenty-three of Lent, I want to focus on Jesus as our hiding place. Scripture describes two kinds of hiding places: one found in the Lord (Psalm 17:8, Psalm 27:5, Psalm 31:20, Psalm 32:7, Psalm 143:9, as examples), and the other, a darker and more self-created and fear-based refuge, where "we have made a lie our refuge and falsehood our hiding place." (Isaiah 28:15). Think of all the myriad ways we try to hide and the things we do to cover ourselves with "fig leaves" like Adam and Eve in the Garden. Alcohol and drugs are emotional hiding places. Pornography is our way of having the feeling of intimacy without the connection, and therefore the commitment, the effort, or the potential loss. We "zone" out into television shows that become more real to us than reality. We seek fun in the worldly sense to distract us from ourselves. Our friends are often more connected to us through the internet than face-to-face, where we are able to see and touch, and feel. When we are face-to-face, we smile and say everything is fine even when it isn't; we won't tell anyone how we feel, or what we need. We won't admit if someone has hurt us or tell them why we were hurt, under the guise of "not upsetting anyone" and "not causing a problem." We are much more likely to simply shut down the relationship than face a conflict and resolve it. And where is Jesus in all this running and avoiding? Psalm 139 tells us there is no hiding from God. "If I say, 'Surely the darkness will hide me and the light become night around me,' even the darkness will not be dark to you;
the night will shine like the day, for darkness is as light to you. (v.11-12).

In spite of everything we do to hide ourselves, Jesus will not leave us alone. To me, that is the meaning of Isaiah 28:17 – Jesus is the living water that will overflow our hiding places. He brings with Him "hail" to destroy the walls of self-protection we build around our hearts, and He floods the isolation we have sought through hiding.

Yes, we have a choice. We can keep on hiding. He'll still stay with us. We can avoid and run away. He'll run beside us. Knowing the consequences, though, and being given a choice, I choose to make Him my "hiding place" – someone I can run to instead of away from, someone to hold me and cover me when my bed is too short and my covers are too small. (v. 20).

To hide ourselves in Jesus is to run to Him in times of trouble for deliverance, yes; however, it is also sheltering ourselves in His arms at all times (Psalm 91) and focusing on what He says is good and right and true (Philippians 4:8). It matters where we take refuge, for in Isaiah 28:18, it calls our false hiding place a covenant with death. The only true protection is found in Jesus, not in the hollow and empty self-protection of our fears, denial, and avoidance. The theme for meditation today is HE IS MY HIDING PLACE.

Notes

Day Twenty-four

For Day Twenty-four of Lent, I want to focus on how immeasurable the love of Christ really is. In Ephesians 3:18-19, Paul prays that we would "grasp how wide and long and high and deep is the love of Christ, and to know this love that surpasses knowledge—that you may be filled to the measure of all the fullness of God." But if His love surpasses knowledge, how can we ever truly grasp it? The answer is found at the foot of the cross.

The coming of Jesus Christ into the world was the ultimate act of love, and as He Himself stated, He has overcome the world (John 16:33). In this context, the word "overcome" means to succeed in dealing with a problem or difficulty, to defeat an opponent, to prevail. Thus, the following concepts are true: 1) The world had a difficulty, a problem that needed to be dealt with; 2) Jesus has an opponent; 3) Jesus prevailed over the opponent; 4) The problem of the world has been successfully resolved. As Christians, we understand these concepts. We see the results of the birth of Christ fulfilled on the cross (the blood payment made for sin) and at the resurrection (the defeat of sin and death, where Jesus prevailed). He came to this world in flesh, in order to be known by us, to reveal love to us, to teach us His truth, and to walk completely in our footsteps in every way, including suffering and death. This is the love of God, "for everyone born of God overcomes the world. This is the victory that has overcome the world" (I John 5:4). Consider, then, the fullness of the story of Jesus Christ, from birth to death to resurrection, as the ultimate in love, and contemplate the magnificent simplicity of His love in the context of the statement, "Love overcomes;" for it is only through His love that we are able to love, to overcome, and to live.

I encourage you to ask Jesus in prayer to take you to the cross, to allow you to share in His experience and to show you what His taking your place truly meant. The theme for meditation today is HE TOOK MY PLACE.

Notes

Day Twenty-five

For Day Twenty-five of Lent, I want to focus on God's abundance. Jesus said, "I have come that they may have life, and have it to the full." (John 10:10). Some have interpreted that Scripture as meaning God will make wealthy or give us material things, but given that Jesus also said, "Blessed are you who are poor, for yours is the kingdom of God" (Luke 6:20), and asked the rich young ruler to give away everything he owned to the poor, it doesn't make sense to think abundance is found in possession or wealth. What He gives us in unlimited abundance are the things our true hearts most deeply desire.

We must make the distinction here between the desires of the flesh and the desires of the heart. "Those who live according to the flesh have their minds set on what the flesh desires; but those who live in accordance with the Spirit have their minds set on what the Spirit desires. The mind governed by the flesh is death, but the mind governed by the Spirit is life and peace. The mind governed by the flesh is hostile to God; it does not submit to God's law, nor can it do so. Those who are in the realm of the flesh cannot please God. You, however, are not in the realm of the flesh but are in the realm of the Spirit, if indeed the Spirit of God lives in you." (Romans 8:5-9). What do we know about what the Spirit desires? Paul gives us a clear picture in Galatians 5:22-23: "the fruit of the Spirit is love, joy, peace, patience, kindness, goodness, faithfulness, gentleness and temperance. Against such things there is no law." All of these things, He gives us in abundance.

In my day by day living, Jesus surrounds me with a bubble of His peace that permeates all of my being. During times of difficulty, He shields me with His truth, so that the arrows of the evil one bounce off of me, allowing me to rejoice even in my suffering (Colossians 1:24). Even when it appears I am on my own, I am never alone, because in His faithfulness, He walks beside me, before me, behind me, and within me. When I make mistakes or sin against Him, His abundant patience, grace, and mercy never fail me, and He never abandons or rejects me, instead gently encouraging me back onto His narrow path. In His goodness, He gives me the freedom to choose Him, rather than compelling my choices or controlling my path.

But love is the one thing, above all else, that we both need and desire, and He adores me. "Love never fails." (I Corinthians 13:8). His love pours out into my heart like endless water onto a desert, filling me and feeding me and enriching me and growing me. The theme for meditation today is HE GIVES ABUNDANTLY.

Notes

Day Twenty-six

For Day Twenty-Six of Lent, I want to talk about fear. As Christians, we spend so much time talking against "physical" sins, like the lust seen in adultery and pornography, the envy and pride seen in comparing ourselves to others and gossiping, or the greed seen in failure to tithe and refusal to use our time to serve others; yet, we continue to live in fear and determine our choices based on fear without any consideration that this is also sin. It is almost like we believe fear is a part of life, a given that we simply have to cope with. Scripture is clear that fear is not of God or from God. For example, I John 4:18 tells us, "There is no fear in love. But perfect love drives out fear, because fear has to do with punishment. The one who fears is not made perfect in love." So fear is sin, no different from any other sin, and through Christ, we have been freed from it.

Although we have been set free from fear, we often continue to choose based on fear. An honest and insightful evaluation of this issue may expose something in our hearts that we do not want to acknowledge, but that needs to be addressed: a persisting belief that we are worthy of judgment and should be punished. John describes a direct relationship between fear, judgment, and love: God is love. Whoever lives in love lives in God, and God in them. This is how love is made complete among us so that we will have confidence on the Day of Judgment: In this world we are like Jesus. (I John 4:16-17). How many of us accept that we have been made like Christ, and reflect Jesus into the world? How many of us love ourselves exactly in the way that God loves us? John proposes an outlandish idea, something that was often done by Jesus and subsequently His followers: we are made perfect in love. John is not saying we can be perfect (get it right or be good enough) or that God demands us to reach perfection (strive to meet the demands of the Law). He is claiming that we ARE made perfect, and it is God's love that makes us perfect.

Paul describes it this way in Romans 8:15: "The Spirit you received does not make you slaves, so that you live in fear again; rather, the Spirit you received brought about your adoption to sonship." As children of God, we do not need to live in fear any longer. Our life is secured by Christ, our judgment is completed on the cross, and no one can take these gifts away from us. If we trust in His truth, and fully live in the embrace of His love, there will be no more room for fear. The theme for meditation today is HE CASTS OUT FEAR.

Notes

Day Twenty-seven

For Day Twenty-seven of Lent, I want to focus on the importance of love. In response to the question, "Which is the greatest commandment?" Jesus replied, "Love the Lord your God with all your heart and with all your soul and with all your mind.' This is the first and greatest commandment. And the second is like it: 'Love your neighbor as yourself.' All the Law and the Prophets hang on these two commandments." (Matthew 22:36-40). These commands are so crucial that Jesus states all of the Law and the Prophets hang on them. One aspect of these two greatest commandments that is rarely discussed is the unstated but understood aspect that in order to follow these two commandments, we must love ourselves.

To love the Creator with all of our heart and soul and mind, we must also love who He created. Self-despising, self-debasement, and shame are all contrary to this command. To hate the creation is to hate the Creator. Loving ourselves does not mean that we aggrandize ourselves or that we become self-centered or self-important. In fact, those responses are Satan's counterfeits to true love of self. Loving ourselves means that we see ourselves as He sees us and love ourselves as He loves us. It means that we value who God created as lovely (because He made us so) and worthy (because He says we are) and precious (because He treats us as such). As a result, we are to treat ourselves with the respect accorded to a child of God. Out of that love, we are able to fully love God and truly love others.

Above all else, His love has the power to transform hearts. We cannot help but be changed by His love. Jesus is the proof of that truth, for it is His love that changed Peter, John, Mary Magdalene, the woman at the well, Paul, and countless others told about in Scripture, as well as innumerable individuals we have never heard of…including me.

"And we all, who with unveiled faces contemplate the Lord's glory, are being transformed into his image with ever-increasing glory, which comes from the Lord, who is the Spirit." (II Corinthians 3:18). The theme for meditation today is HIS LOVE TRANSFORMS.

Notes

Day Twenty-eight

For Day Twenty-eight of Lent, I want to focus on Jesus' instruction to us to love one another as He loves us. At the Last Supper, Jesus said, "A new command I give you: Love one another. As I have loved you, so you must love one another. By this everyone will know that you are my disciples, if you love one another." (John 13:34-35). This was an important enough instruction that Jesus chose to share it at the most intimate, emotional, and substantive moment of His relationship with His disciples.

God's love is the source of all love, so God's love for us is what fuels our love for one another. Love is the sole reason for our creation, both in the sense that it is out of love for us that He created us, made us in His image, and gave us freedom so that we, too, can love; and, in the sense that we are created specifically for this purpose, to share that love and extend that love to others, bringing the Kingdom into the world. We do not exist separate from God. If His love is what created us, we are in essence an extension of that love. But His love for us is not intended to just remain hidden in our hearts. He wants His love to flow out of our lives into the lives of others, to expose those who do not know or understand His love to a small taste of His love, so that they will want to seek Him and know Him.

Paul explains it this way: "Let no debt remain outstanding, except the continuing debt to love one another, for whoever loves others has fulfilled the law. The commandments, 'You shall not commit adultery,' 'You shall not murder,' 'You shall not steal,' 'You shall not covet,' and whatever other command there may be, are summed up in this one command: 'Love your neighbor as yourself.' Love does no harm to a neighbor. Therefore love is the fulfillment of the law." (Romans 13:8-10).

One of the most important questions we can ask the Lord as we walk through our daily lives is, "What is the loving thing to do?" For, "If I speak in the tongues of men and of angels, but have not love, I am a noisy gong or a clanging cymbal. And if I have prophetic powers, and understand all mysteries and all knowledge, and if I have all faith, so as to remove mountains, but have not love, I am nothing. If I give away all I have, and if I deliver up my body to be burned, but have not love, I gain nothing." (I Corinthians 13:1-3). The theme for meditation today is HIS LOVE IS POURED OUT.

Notes

Day Twenty-nine

For Day Twenty-nine of Lent, I want to talk about standing firm and strong. The enemy, the father of lies (John 8:44), attempts to undermine our foundation by using circumstances and behavior, both our actions and the actions of others, as evidence that lies we believe are actually true. As a result, the lies we believe often *feel* true to us. Those lie beliefs in our hearts about ourselves, about God, and about others influence our responses, and the more we respond based on the lies, the more evidence the enemy has to use against us. For example, if I believe I am not good enough, the comments of others gain a tremendous amount of power. I will fear rejection or judgment from others, and will acquiesce to please them. As a result, I develop bitterness and resentment toward others because of the perceived power they have over me (which they do not actually have, because no one can "make" me feel or do anything). The enemy is quick to shame and condemn me for my anger; thus, I feel the judgment and rejection that I originally feared. Similarly, if I believe I am worthless, I will fear being abandoned or being mistreated (because I deserve to be mistreated) and I will self-protect, closing and hardening my heart, which in turn creates the exact thing I feared – I am now alone. Satan is very quick to say "I told you so."

What we need to stand firm, then, is truth. "Stand firm then, with the belt of truth buckled around your waist, with the breastplate of righteousness in place, and with your feet fitted with the readiness that comes from the gospel of peace. In addition to all this, take up the shield of faith, with which you can extinguish all the flaming arrows of the evil one. Take the helmet of salvation and the sword of the Spirit, which is the word of God." (Ephesians 6:14-17). When we know the truth in our hearts, no matter what the circumstances are, we will stand certain and strong on that rock, and walk in freedom. By the same token, if we feel shaken, we can know that we are missing some truth, and can seek the Lord to speak or reveal the truth we need. We can live in freedom from fear. In order to live fearlessly, we need to remain in constant connection to Jesus, always seeking His truth to be spoken to our hearts, walking with Him as our partner in all things and at all times. Paul completes his description of the armor of God with this admonition: "pray in the Spirit on all occasions with all kinds of prayers" (v. 18). Jesus desires communion with us, and if we will take the time to listen, He will guide us to the truth.

"Truly my soul finds rest in God; my salvation comes from him. Truly he is my rock and my salvation; he is my fortress, I will never be shaken." (Psalm 62:1-2). The theme for meditation today is HE IS MY ROCK.

Notes

Day Thirty

For Day Thirty of Lent, I want to talk about what constitutes our legacy. A legacy is what is passed down to us like a bequest or an inheritance. We may feel as if what defines us is our earthly family, and that how they see us, how they treat us, what they teach us about ourselves and life, and how they act is our legacy – our inheritance. But our family history does not define us, and no person determines our identity. Instead, Scripture tells us our legacy: "we are heirs—heirs of God and co-heirs with Christ (Romans 8:17), and, again states, "So you are no longer a slave, but a son, and if a son, then an heir through God." (Galatians 4:7). We know that, "In His great mercy he has given us new birth into a living hope through the resurrection of Jesus Christ from the dead, and into an inheritance that can never perish, spoil or fade." (I Peter 1:3-4), and we know that Jesus "has qualified (us) to share in the inheritance of His holy people in the kingdom of light." (Colossians 1:12). My legacy, my inheritance, and my identity is that I am a child of God.

God is our True Parent. So our true legacy is what God says about us, how He sees us as made in His image reflecting aspects of His character and nature, how He has loved us beyond even our understanding, and every truth He teaches us. Our inheritance is the Kingdom of God, not at some future time or in some future place, but right here and right now, in our hearts. We are His precious children, beloved and desired more than all else in creation. What an incredible legacy!

"I pray that the eyes of your heart may be enlightened in order that you may know the hope to which he has called you, the riches of his glorious inheritance in his holy people, and his incomparably great power for us who believe." (Ephesians 1:18-19). The theme for meditation today is HE IS MY LEGACY.

Notes

Day Thirty-one

For Day Thirty-one of Lent, I want to focus on the hope we have in Jesus. It is the hope of glory – but it isn't only a future hope. It is the hope of redemption – but it isn't only hope for our souls. It is the hope for eternity – but it isn't only a hope for heaven. The hope in Christ that is the most unexpected and the most astounding is the hope we find in the here and now, in each and every moment of our lives. In times of enjoyment and happiness, we can share in His laughter with us, and His warm and peaceful presence adding to our joy. In the midst of the worst times in our lives, during our times of loss or trauma or pain, we have the hope that comes from His arms holding us tightly, His loving voice speaking encouragement and comfort, His truth flowing into our hearts bringing healing to the wounds, His strong sword and shield defending us and protecting us from the enemy and fighting by our sides for our sakes.

With Him, we have the assurance of His stabilizing influence in our lives, and we have confidence in the unchanging nature of His truth. These certainties bring us peace: "peace with God through our Lord Jesus Christ. Through him we have also obtained access by faith into this grace in which we stand, and we rejoice in hope of the glory of God...and hope does not disappoint, because God's love has been poured into our hearts through the Holy Spirit who has been given to us." (Romans 5:1-2, 5). Without Him, trying to face this world on our own, there is no hope. Hopelessness assumes He is not present, He is not alive, He is not with us, He is not for us, and He is not involved. Hopelessness is like a black, bubbling river that flows in our hearts. Sometimes it flows above ground where we can see it, and sometimes it flows underground, hidden from our consciousness, but whether we are aware of it or not, hopelessness undermines our foundation and erodes the ground on which we stand.

Hopelessness comes when we put our confidence in something else besides Him. We may hope in people in our lives, but they will disappoint us, even if they love us and we love them. We may hope in some particular circumstance working out, but it may or may not work in our favor or as we want. We may hope in those in authority over us, but as human beings they will surely fail.

Our hope is in Him and in Him alone. Isaiah 49:23 states: "Then you will know that I am the LORD; those who hope in me will not be disappointed." The theme for meditation today is HE IS MY HOPE.

Notes

Day Thirty-two

For Day Thirty-two of Lent, I want to focus on the acceptance of Christ. Our God does not come to us with demands, expectations, and lists of things we must do to gain acceptance from Him. He is not a God Who sits back with folded arms waiting for us to get it right so we can reach Him where He is. No! Our God left His throne and came here for us, with the specific purpose of restoring us to Him. He pursues us before we have ever even heard His name. He wants us, no matter our condition or sin or circumstances. He meets us wherever we are, and accepts us as we are. He does not add to our burden; He relieves our burden and lightens our load. He says, "Come to me, all you who are weary and burdened, and I will give you rest. Take my yoke upon you and learn from me, for I am gentle and humble in heart, and you will find rest for your souls. For my yoke is easy and my burden is light." (Matthew 11:28-30). He loves us, even as we reject Him, and patiently stands with us to gently restore us, just like He did for Peter, who denied knowing Jesus three times, but Jesus still sought Peter out and asked him three times, "do you love me?" (John 21:15-17), in order to help Peter let go of his shame.

Being accepted freely by Christ does not mean we have no responsibility or accountability for our choices. Scripture in both Old and New Testaments is clear that our choices have consequences (Deuteronomy 30:11-20; Proverbs 11:18, 22:8; 2 Corinthians 9:6, Galatians 6:7-8, James 3:18). Consequences are built into the fabric of creation, and even the laws of physics express that actions produce reactions. The reason God created such a system was out of love for us. Imagine for a moment what our lives would be like if our actions produced no predictable results. How could we ever learn what is beneficial and what is harmful? Without resulting consequences, we would be repeating the same harmful actions over and over again, but never learning. However, Satan has perverted personal responsibility, which is stated as "I acknowledge making a poor choice and I will make a different choice next time," and turned it into shame, which says, "I am bad." And what hope is there if my very being is bad?

Shame would tell us that we aren't good enough for God, or we aren't worth Him loving us, but Scripture refutes that lie, saying "God shows his love for us in that while we were still sinners, Christ died for us." (Romans 5:8). It is freeing to know there is nothing we can do to earn His love, or to lose it or change it. The theme for meditation today is HE ACCEPTS ME AS I AM.

Notes

Day Thirty-three

For Day Thirty-three of Lent, I want to talk about perseverance in fighting the good fight. Perseverance is esteemed in Scripture as a characteristic which produces spiritual maturity and growth in us, as shown in the following examples: "Let perseverance finish its work so that you may be mature and complete, not lacking anything" (James 1:4); "Blessed is the one who perseveres under trial because, having stood the test, that person will receive the crown of life that the Lord has promised to those who love him" (James 1:12); "we count as blessed those who have persevered" (James 5:11); "we know that suffering produces perseverance; perseverance, character; and character, hope." (Romans 5:3). We are instructed to persevere in the fight: "let us throw off everything that hinders and the sin that so easily entangles. And let us run with perseverance the race marked out for us… Consider him who endured such opposition from sinners, so that you will not grow weary and lose heart." (Hebrews 12:1, 3). Our call to persevere is based on the example set by Christ, who endured the scorn and shame of the cross, and we are strengthened by the Holy Spirit within us to finish the fight.

The best example of perseverance in fighting the good fight I have ever witnessed was my son, Cody. In spite of a debilitating illness that stole his strength, his legs, and his breath, he knew who he was and he knew why he was here. He never was hopeless or despairing, always knowing who carried him – and who breathed for him. Cody wasn't in denial; he was aware that his body was dying; but as far as he was concerned, he was already in the Kingdom, so it didn't make much difference one way or the other to him if his body betrayed him. He was fully alive, and he lived his life to the fullest. His joy and peace in the face of great physical struggle touched many other lives, and every struggle he faced was redeemed.

For his funeral, Cody chose II Timothy 4:7 for the Scripture: "I have fought the good fight, I have finished the race, I have kept the faith." Truly, he exemplified this verse in every moment of his life. If you are struggling, no matter the nature of the struggle, don't give up. Remember who carries you and who gives you breath. Run the race to the finish. Fight the good fight. Keep the faith. The theme for meditation today is HE CARRIES ME.

Notes

Day Thirty-four

For Day Thirty-four of Lent, I want to talk about the Kingdom of God. The teachings of Jesus are so radical, so completely and wildly different from the expected and from how we view the world, that it is easy for us to tell ourselves He didn't really mean it. To gain my life I must lose it? Blessed are the poor? Take the least important seat? Those who exalt themselves will be humbled and the humble exalted? Blessed are those who are persecuted and insulted? To be great you must be a servant? Love your enemies? The thoughts and motives of our hearts matter more than our actions? The Kingdom is like the tiniest seed? Do not store up treasures on earth but store up treasures in heaven? The last will be first and the first last? Whatever you do for the least of these you do for Him? Those who serve will recline at the table and be served by the Master? Forgive seventy times seven? Blessed are those who mourn? Reconcile with others before offering a gift to God? Sell what you have and give to the poor? The greatest will be the least? The Kingdom of God as described by Jesus is a series of paradoxes that turn our worldly thinking upside down.

Jesus talks about entering the Kingdom of God, not in terms of going to heaven when we die, but in terms of living in the Kingdom in the here and now. We are welcomed as part of His Kingdom through accepting Christ and believing His truth; however, living in the Kingdom now means certain things are true, and all of them are counterintuitive. So in order to live in the Kingdom now, we must lose our perspective and adopt His counterintuitive one. For example, we firmly believe that by worrying, we can avoid problems and protect ourselves. However, Jesus taught, "Do not worry about your life…Can any of you by worrying add a single hour to your life?" (Matthew 6:25, 34). In order to live in the Kingdom, we need to choose the opposite of whatever fear and worry tells us to do. We also need to let go of our illusion of creating safety by shutting down our feelings, by avoiding dealing with problem issues, and by building walls against hurt, because Scripture tells us, "the peace of God, which transcends all understanding, will guard your hearts and your minds in Christ Jesus" (Philippians 4:7). Once again, our self-perspective would say that makes no sense, that peace cannot be a protection for us. The backwards and upside down perspective of the Kingdom of God is found in His view of choosing the easy way vs. taking the harder road. We see the wide, broad road, and think, easy must be good and hard must be bad. He sees that same road and says, "Enter through the narrow gate. For wide is the gate and broad is the road that leads to destruction, and many enter through it. But small is the gate and narrow the road that leads to life, and only a few find it" (Matthew 7:13-14).

Endeavor to live counterintuitively. Adopting the perspective of the Kingdom and dropping the worldly view, even though it goes against everything we intuit, is a life of freedom, hope, and peace. As Jesus said, "You do not belong to the world, but I have chosen you out of the world" (John 15:19). What else would we expect from our God, Who instead of conquering evil through power and destruction, came to earth as a man, humbled Himself, and died? And yes, He really DID mean it. The theme for meditation today is HE CHANGES EVERYTHING.

Notes

Palm Sunday

For Palm Sunday, I want to focus on Jesus' victory. The Jewish people celebrated Jesus' entry into Jerusalem, expecting the promised Messiah to be a triumphant King to come and lead them to victory over the Romans, but Jesus had so much more for them. They wanted to be liberated from the Romans, but He wanted their complete freedom from death and separation from God. They wanted a worldly king, and He offered them an eternal King. They wanted Him to reign over them in Jerusalem, but He wanted to invite all into His Kingdom and to bring His Kingdom to the whole earth.

They were so excited to see Him enter Jerusalem like a victorious King, but then things did not go as they expected, and when He was arrested and then crucified, everyone fled, even those closest to Him who were called disciples. We might be tempted to judge their response, but we need to remember as we read these stories that we are just like them. Do we rejoice and praise Him when everything is going smoothly, and when things don't go as we want them to, do we flee and hide, or reject Him, just like the disciples and all the people who were cheering His triumphant entry into Jerusalem? Do we expect Him to fix things in our circumstances, while He is seeking to transform us into His image with ever-increasing glory (II Corinthians 3:18)? Do we ask Him for worldly treasures like successful outcomes, greater status, or power and wealth, when what He wants to give us is His Kingdom within our hearts (Matthew 6:19-21)? Do we pray and serve for our own benefit, or to be seen doing it by others, rather than follow His example and pray and serve out of love for the benefit of others (Matthew 6:2-6)? Do we believe in Him out of fear, as our ticket to enter Heaven when we die, or out of obligation like we owe Him something quid pro quo, or do we love Him with our whole hearts, as He loves us (John 15:9)? He has so much more for us as well.

Today begins the week termed the Passion, from the Greek and Latin meaning suffering, of Christ. I encourage you to prepare your hearts anew for His message, and to open yourself fully to celebrate His *true* victory. The theme for meditation today is HE IS MY KING.

Notes

Day Thirty-five

For Day Thirty-five of Lent, I want to talk about Jesus' fierceness. His first action after He entered Jerusalem was to go to the Temple. What He found there was corruption, hypocrisy, selfishness, self-righteousness, power, control, and abuse of His people. His response to what He found was to turn over the tables of those making money off of the command to bring sacrifice to God (Matthew 21:12-13), confront the hypocrisy He saw (Matthew 23), and teach the true nature of the Kingdom of God (Matthew 21:28-32, Matthew 21:33-44, Matthew 22:1-14). Knowing He would anger the powers that be at that time (Matthew 21:45-46), He stood for what was true and did what was right. He calls us to do the same, with His help and partnership.

Sometimes we hesitate to take a fierce stand for truth, in fear of appearing judgmental or harsh or insensitive or exclusive, all of which are frowned upon in our society. Accountability and personal responsibility have given way to viewing ourselves as victims and preferring to blame others rather than looking within for growth; fairness has taken the place of justice; and, the postmodern belief in relative truth has insisted that there are no absolutes, leaving us nothing to stand on. We don't want to risk offending anyone, but remember, Paul called the cross itself an "offense" (Galatians 5:11). I would say that if Jesus came today, He would be crucified again, just not on the cross but in the court of public opinion and social media, because He would still take the same fierce stance for truth today that He took in the Temple in Jerusalem. A question for us to answer is, who will we imitate – our culture or our Lord?

Are we fierce in our defense of our Lord? How do we respond when we hear others disparage the character of God or lie about His nature? Do we confront hypocrisy where we see it and defend His honor and character when it is falsely presented? Before we can confront hypocrisy in this world, we must first confront the lies and hypocrisy within us. Will we honestly and fiercely face our own duplicity and allow Jesus to cull our own lie beliefs and replace them with His truth? Do we stand up for truth, in ourselves as well as with others, no matter what it might cost us? Will we live in the freedom He has died to provide for us, or will we accept the status quo? The theme for meditation today is HE IS FIERCE.

Notes

Day Thirty-six

For Day Thirty-six of Lent, I want to focus on spreading the gospel. Our lives have a lot more impact on others than our words, so as we seek to share Jesus with others, searching our own lives first and deepening our own relationship with Christ is the most important step we can take toward witnessing effectively. We must know Jesus – not know about Him, but know Him personally through experience and interaction – before we can influence others to come to Him. If we truly follow Jesus' example, He fed people, healed people, and connected with people before He taught people; in other words, He loved and served before He led.

Now, I am not saying that sharing our love for Jesus is something we "have to do" for others, or that it is "how we behave" around others, because that quickly becomes a list of expectations and rules for us to follow, binding us once again to the Law. However, if we understand the nature of "fruit" – and Jesus tells us others will know us by our fruit (Matthew 7:16) – fruit is what grows naturally on a tree or bush based on the nature of that plant. Thus, being who God created us to be and fully expressing that nature will speak more about Jesus to others than anything we could possibly say.

Does your life reflect the aspect or aspects of God that He has placed within you? If not, what scheme of the enemy is obscuring that wonderful nature, and what truth do you need from Jesus to remove the lies that are hiding your light? "You are the light of the world. A town built on a hill cannot be hidden. Neither do people light a lamp and put it under a bowl. Instead they put it on its stand, and it gives light to everyone in the house." (Matthew 5:14-15). When we live fully as who He created us, the light that flows from our hearts draws people to Jesus.

One of the most powerful statements I have ever heard made about Cody was said by a nonbeliever, who said, "I've never been sure there is a God, but Cody makes me believe there is One." Cody engendered this response, not by talking to this nonbeliever about God, but simply by living his life being who God made him to be in spite of his difficult circumstances, and letting the light of Jesus shine out of his heart.

"In the same way, let your light shine before others" (Matthew 5:16). Others will naturally want to know what it is that is making your heart sing. The theme for meditation today is HE IS MY SONG.

Notes

Day Thirty-seven

For Day Thirty-seven of Lent, I want to talk about the coming of Christ. Lent is designed to prepare our hearts in anticipation of Easter, the most important and most transformational event that has ever happened. But I would like to suggest that we use this opportunity to also prepare our hearts for His return, because establishing His Kingdom on earth as it is in heaven is what we are called to usher in. We don't want to be the bride attendants who were not ready for the bridegroom's arrival (Matthew 25:1-13). In addition to teaching us to be ready and prepared, this parable also shows us that we cannot rely on the preparation of others to equip us for the bridegroom's return. We must have our own "oil" (a deep and intimate relationship with the Holy Spirit) because when the time comes, we will not be able to use the oil of others for ourselves. Therefore, it is simply not enough to go to church every Sunday and listen to the sermon, or even to go to Sunday school or small group or Bible study for the teaching. We are instructed and called into personal intimacy, which means connection, conversation, and communion. Those elements require moment-by-moment intentionality to build and establish in our hearts.

We are not meant to passively wait for His coming, looking to the sky for the light from the east while we keep on going with business as usual. Once the Kingdom of God is in our hearts, we are intended to actively promote His Kingdom being established here as it flows out of our hearts into others and into our sphere of influence. Remember, "The Lord is not slow to fulfill his promise as some count slowness, but is patient toward you, not wishing that any should perish, but that all should reach repentance." (II Peter 3:9). Like every other story that is told in Scripture, God has made us partners with Him in setting the stage for Christ's return. Our greatest joy is found in participating in His Kingdom come. The theme for meditation today is HE IS COMING.

Ready yourselves. Each of the next four days marks an incredibly significant step toward our salvation and fulfillment. I encourage you to prepare today for what is to come, and ponder deeply each day of Christ's passion because all of it was done for you.

Notes

Day Thirty-eight

For Day Thirty-eight of Lent, I want to focus on Jesus suffering. His suffering had many elements, happened at multiple times, and took on many forms. In the garden at Gethsemane, Jesus faced the anticipation of great physical suffering, the intense pain of being betrayed, and the awareness that everyone who said they loved Him did and would abandon Him. He described His feelings as "my soul is overwhelmed with sorrow to the point of death" (Matthew 26:38). He asked His closest friends to sit with Him while He prayed, but even those closest to Him could not manage to stay awake and pray with Him or for Him. When they could not manage to be there for Him, He enlisted them to pray for themselves, that they would not falter; yet, they could not stay awake for even their own sakes, and He was left to pray alone.

In Gethsemane, He experienced exactly what we experience when faced with our own fear, during our own loss and trauma, when we feel alone and lonely, and when we are abandoned and betrayed. The consequences of loss, isolation, abandonment, betrayal, and suffering are known and intimately experienced by Him, so much so that His very soul was overwhelmed with its sorrow. What we see in Jesus' response to these consequences can help us through our own experiences. First, He acknowledged His pain; He didn't avoid it or deny it. Immediately, He turned to His Father for help and comfort. He asked for what He wanted, while accepting God's will as the expression of His deepest heart's desire. Finally, He stood up and faced what was to come with confidence (v. 46).

I was struck that, when the betrayer came, Jesus called him "friend." (v. 50).

We do not love a God Who sits in the heavenlies, looks down on our plight in pity, and corrects us or punishes us for getting it wrong. We love our Jesus, Who stood where we stand, Who felt what we feel, Who shared these experiences with us – all so that we could fully know Him, relate to Him, connect with Him, and so that we can be free. "It is for freedom that Christ has set us free." (Galatians 5:1). The theme for meditation today is HE SUFFERED FOR ME.

Notes

Day Thirty-nine

For Day Thirty-nine of Lent, I want to focus on the cross. Jesus' suffering took on a new form at His trial, scourging, and crucifixion. In addition to the deep emotional pain of abandonment, betrayal, and grief, His pain was now inflicted on His body. The payment for our sin was meted out in every welt, every thorn, and every nail He suffered. Along with this physical agony, the humiliation of carrying our shame was the weight of the cross on His tortured shoulders.

It is difficult for us to have a conversation about suffering. We prefer avoidance to facing suffering, because we don't want to experience any pain ourselves. We treat suffering as the problem, and miss the actual problem that the pain is attempting to identify for us. We choose repression, denial, and pretense over honestly confronting and dealing with the cause of our suffering, believing on some level that we shouldn't have to suffer. However, I would contend that none of these justifications or rationalizations can withstand the presence of the cross of Christ. Jesus took suffering and bore it in His flesh, graphically displayed, literally hung out in public for all to see. He didn't view suffering as something to be avoided, and He didn't worry about upsetting even those closest to Him with the reality of suffering. He said, "Here it is: the consequences of sin displayed in my blood and in wounds on my own body." No sugar coating there, and certainly no avoidance. Jesus carried that reality all the way up Calvary.

However, our experience of suffering depends greatly on our interpretation of the suffering. Do we see it as God's punishment, shameful and deserved? Do we give it tremendous power over us, such that we face it with fear? Do we approach it as a victim, as if our choice is removed? If those responses dictate our view, suffering for us will indeed be a horrible experience. However, if suffering is simply a signal that something is wrong that needs to be addressed; if suffering, whether physical or emotional, is our personal warning system to indicate we have something we need to share with Jesus to receive His peace, His presence, and His truth; then suffering, under that understanding of its purpose, loses its power and subsequent fear, and carries with it no shame, relieving us of the lie-based interpretations and their consequences while providing us with a redemptive response to suffering just as Paul described in Romans 5:1-4: "Therefore, since we have been justified through faith, we have peace with God through our Lord Jesus Christ, through whom we have gained access by faith into this grace in which we now stand. And we boast in the hope of the glory of God. Not only so, but we also glory in our sufferings, because we know that suffering produces perseverance; perseverance, character; and character, hope."

"It is finished." (John 19:30). The ultimate payment for sin – death – which up until the cross was paid by us, is now paid in full by Jesus' death. *Paid in full.* The fear and shame of sin have no more weight for us because of the cross, freeing us to see suffering for what it is: an opportunity to turn to the Lord for help. "I consider that our present sufferings are not worth comparing with the glory that will be revealed in us." (Romans 8:18). The theme for meditation today is HE DIED FOR ME.

Notes

Day Forty

For Day Forty of Lent, I want to focus on silence. When I imagine the pall of darkness that must have fallen over the land while Jesus descended to hell to battle against the enemy and death (Ephesians 4:8-10), it brings my heart and mind to silence – not the peaceful silence of sitting in the arms of Jesus being loved and held and comforted; not the silence of watching a sunset at the end of a beautiful day witnessing God's glorious creation – but the empty silence of nothingness.

I see the Romans and Jewish leaders going on with their affairs and machinations, oblivious to the nothingness – they would not sense it, because they were always in the darkness and did not witness the light or recognize it when it was among them. I see Peter, John, Mary, Mary Magdalene, and all of the other disciples sitting in the weight of the emptiness, burdened by the realization of their loss and the shame of their abandonment of Jesus. I see them wondering, "What now?" and feeling like their lives were over. I see hopelessness and despair, anguish and grief; they too were blinded to what Jesus was doing, even though He had told them what would happen.

I see the desolation and lifeless void left in His absence. I imagine nature itself "groaning as in the pains of childbirth" (Romans 8:22) as it waited. I imagine all movement ceased: no breath of wind, no sound of birds singing, no more of the ebb and flow of life. "For the creation waits in eager expectation for the children of God to be revealed." (Romans 8:19).

I imagine the agony and anticipation in Heaven, as if a collective breath was being held. I imagine the heart of the Father, and remembering my sorrow the day after Cody's death, I recognize I felt only an infinitesimal amount of the agony He experienced.

For meditation, I ask you to silently be aware of the life or death fight that was raging between Jesus and Satan in hell on this day. I ask you to consider our own blindness to its significance. I encourage you to ask Jesus for spiritual eyes with which is see, and a heart to understand. I did not choose a theme for this meditation, as I believe silence is appropriate for this day.

Notes

Easter

The ground heaved and shook. The guards stood paralyzed. The Roman seal crumbled to dust. The massive grave stone became like a feather on a breeze. The light that had left the world on Friday returned, flooding the darkness and breathing life into our emptiness.

Hallelujah! He is risen! He who was dead is alive! "Death has been swallowed up in victory. Where, O death, is your victory? Where, O death, is your sting? Thanks be to God! He gives us the victory through our Lord Jesus Christ." (I Corinthians 15: 54-57). What an amazing image: Death has been swallowed up. That which was the consumer of all was consumed. The recompense that our sin laid claim against us was null and void, and everything it wrought was rendered defeated.

With Paul, "I pray that the eyes of your heart may be enlightened in order that you may know the hope to which he has called you, the riches of his glorious inheritance in his holy people, and his incomparably great power for us who believe. That power is the same as the mighty strength he exerted when he raised Christ from the dead and seated him at his right hand in the heavenly realms, far above all rule and authority, power and dominion, and every name that is invoked, not only in the present age but also in the one to come." (Ephesians 1:18-21).

Our glorious inheritance is not a doctrine, not a rulebook by which to live, not concepts and ideas to make us feel better, not a set of expectations to live up to, not a nice story to teach us life lessons or morals – the riches we receive is a love relationship with the very real, very present, LIVING GOD. "Worthy is the Lamb, who was slain, to receive power and wealth and wisdom and strength and honor and glory and praise!" (Revelation 5:12). The theme for meditation today is HE IS ALIVE.

Notes

Conclusion

As the 40 days of Lent draws to a close, I want to conclude this wilderness journey by sharing who Jesus is to me. Jesus asked the disciples, "Who do people say the Son of man is?" They responded with what people had said about Jesus. He then asked them, "Who do you say I am?" (Matthew 16:13-16). It was Peter who named Jesus honestly for who he knew Jesus to be, and in response Jesus gave Peter his real name and revealed his purpose. It is one thing to know *about* Jesus, which I can read in Scripture and glean from hearing others talk about Him. It is something completely different to *know* Him personally, authentically, intimately, and truthfully.

My answer to the question Jesus posed to Peter is, "Jesus, you are my real Daddy. You are the center of my life. You are my Savior, my rescuer, my healer, my best friend, my first love. You are my comfort in my grief. You are my strength, and my shield and defender. You are my Redeemer. You are my partner. You are my peace. You are my everything."

Have you ever noticed how different the night sky looks depending on where you are standing to observe it? Out in the wilderness, the night sky is practically alight with billions upon billions of stars, so many you could not begin to count them, and the vastness of space is unveiled before your eyes in its twinkling bright majesty and glory. However, in a more populated area, where man-made lights, such as street lights, billboards, lights in buildings, porch lights, and headlights, distract and drown out the stars, only the brightest stars can be seen, and you might imagine the night sky is sparsely populated by a few specific points of light. In a large urban area, along with the ambient light, you have large buildings blocking your view of the sky, such that you might believe the night sky is just tiny glimpses of postage stamp sized squares with no real light in it. Of course, if the sky where you are standing is covered in a blanket of dark clouds, you might believe the night sky is a black abyss, empty and void. Yet, the reality of the night sky is always the same; only your perception of it changes.

The same is true of how we view God: how we perceive Him depends on where we are standing. When we stand solidly in His truth and focus our eyes on Him, without distractions cluttering our vision or doubt creeping in to block our view or the cloak of the enemy's lies to blanket our head, we can see Him in the vastness of His love, and the beauty and wonder of His glory. His light can guide our steps even in the darkest of times. And although we might not be able to comprehend everything we see, like a child searching the night sky and trying to count the countless stars, we can know HIM because He has revealed Himself to us in Christ, and through Jesus we can "grasp how wide and long and high and deep" is His love, "and to know this love that surpasses knowledge" so that we can be "filled to the measure of all the fullness of God" (Ephesians 3:18-19).

As I stand looking in awe at the fullness of the night sky from the back deck of my cabin in the mountains, I am struck by the truth that my God individually created each and every magnificent star in His own hands and placed each in the sky Himself. He stretched out what I see as the night sky, and knows intimately every detail beyond what my eyes can even see – each planet, each asteroid, each distance, each movement, each speck of dust. This same God, Who created the heavens and the earth, formed me down to every gene and chromosome and cell, and knows everything there is to know about me, from the aspects of His nature that He placed in me that create my unique spirit to the count of the number of hairs on my head (Luke 12:7).

"You have searched me, LORD,
    and you know me.
You know when I sit and when I rise;
    you perceive my thoughts from afar.

You discern my going out and my lying down;
  you are familiar with all my ways.
Before a word is on my tongue
  you, LORD, know it completely.
You hem me in behind and before,
  and you lay your hand upon me.
Such knowledge is too wonderful for me,
  too lofty for me to attain.
Where can I go from your Spirit?
  Where can I flee from your presence?
If I go up to the heavens, you are there;
  if I make my bed in the depths, you are there.
If I rise on the wings of the dawn,
  if I settle on the far side of the sea,
  even there your hand will guide me,
  your right hand will hold me fast.
If I say, 'Surely the darkness will hide me
  and the light become night around me,'
  even the darkness will not be dark to you;
  the night will shine like the day,
  for darkness is as light to you.
For you created my inmost being;
  you knit me together in my mother's womb.
I praise you because I am fearfully and wonderfully made;
  your works are wonderful,
  I know that full well.
My frame was not hidden from you
  when I was made in the secret place,
  when I was woven together in the depths of the earth.
Your eyes saw my unformed body;
  all the days ordained for me were written in your book
  before one of them came to be.
How precious to me are your thoughts, God!
  How vast is the sum of them!

Were I to count them,
    they would outnumber the grains of sand—
    when I awake, I am still with you. (Psalm 139:1-18).

As amazement, humility, and deep gratitude fill my heart and lift up my soul, I know in my heart that I want to stay solidly and firmly standing on His truth each and every moment, ridding my eyes from the distraction and clutter of the stuff of the world and the lies of the enemy. I want to "fix (my) eyes on Jesus" (Psalm 141:8, II Corinthians 4:18, Hebrews 12:1-3) so that I can see Him as He is. "For now we see only a reflection as in a mirror; then we shall see face to face. Now I know in part; then I shall know fully, even as I am fully known." (I Corinthians 13:12).

I have mentioned several times over these 40 days of meditations the importance of communication and communion with Jesus as a foundation for an intimate relationship (as it is with any relationship), and encouraged listening to the Lord in prayer to allow Him to bring truth to your hearts. I pray these writings have motivated you to pursue this kind of intimate connection with Jesus, and that the opportunity for quiet meditation and solitude has afforded you some space and time to listen for His voice.

I am often asked for direction and assistance in learning to hear the Lord's voice, and for how to discern His voice from all of the other inner noise that we experience. Apparently, we have a deep longing for silence and listening in prayer, but since it has not been discussed in many churches for a long time, some may think that this is a new or semi-new concept, something arising out of a sort of modern humanistic spiritualism. They would be in error. Ever heard the saying, "Everything old is new again"?

The early church knew the power of the presence of God. Early church fathers, particularly in the Eastern regions of Christian expansion, practiced what is called "Hesychasm." From the Greek word, *hesychia*, meaning stillness, quiet, silence and rest, this term refers to going to a place of solitude, specifically within one's own heart, and sitting in stillness and quiet to listen to the voice of God and receive from His presence. The term ultimately grew into our English word, hermit, for someone who lives a solitary existence, but in the early church it had more of a connotation of inner solitude, a quietness of the heart and mind that allowed you to be connected intimately with Jesus. As early as the fourth century, this term is found in writings of the early Christians, and these writing suggest it existed as a practice in even earlier times. We can hope that what was once lost has now been found.

I am not a fan of lists of rules or instructions that assume there is one way to do something, in this case because I believe it limits God into a very tiny box of our own experiences, and does not take into account the vast individual differences God has created in each of us. However, in an effort to give a starting point and help those new to the idea of listening to Jesus in our hearts, I want to offer some basic "guidelines" here.

Once you accept that hearing Jesus speak in your heart is possible, open your heart and mind to the manner in which He desires to speak to you. He can use images (internal visions) or pictures to convey His truth; He can speak in words your spirit can hear within; He can leave impressions in your heart and mind, concepts you have not considered or new perceptions that you have not seen before; He can use colors and symbols to convey His presence; He can use Scripture and make it come alive for you in order to teach truth; He can touch your heart in a way that leaves a genuine physical impression of His love. This list is not intended to be complete, but instead is a starting point, an offering for consideration as possibilities.

Begin by quieting your mind. Everyone accomplishes this in their own way, but some suggestions would be to focus on a particular question or thought, to bring up a meaningful memory that has significant emotion still attached to it, or to meditate using breathing and even music to bring calm to your mind. Some early writings suggest repeating over and over again the name of Jesus, or a simple prayer such as "Jesus, have mercy on me." These suggestions came later (6th century and beyond), possibly due to an increasing loss of connection or difficulty in knowing how to become intimate with Jesus. I imagine the concept of the repetitive prayer was mainly about ways to quiet the mind, as the mind can only focus on one thought at a time, and if you force the mind to repeat a thought it can allow you to truly enter into your heart. However, this became ritualized and lost its purpose in later centuries.

Then, consider what you would want to know from Jesus or what you want to talk to Him about. All topics are open to you, and so is simply sitting with Him and feeling His love for you. As I presented in the meditation for Day Nineteen, I recommend asking Him to tell you about Himself, because I believe the two questions we all need to know the answers to are, "Who is God really?" and, "Who does God say I am?" Before we can know who we are, we must first know our Creator, so start with asking about God. After learning about Who He is, next ask Him to tell you who He created you to be. One way to ask this question is to ask Jesus for your "new name" (Revelation 2:17). Knowing this truth from your God is the only way to truly know who you are, and the certain knowledge spoken with authority by your Creator frees you to be fully who you were created to be.

At this point, it is important to understand that things can get in the way of our hearing. Some of these things that can interfere include our preconceived religious ideas; lie beliefs we have from our early experiences about ourselves, about life, and about God; and, our own fear or shame of coming face to face with God. So, if at first you do not experience any presence when you begin to listen, don't be concerned or feel like you have not done it "right." Instead, ask Jesus to reveal, meaning bring into the light, what is in the way. Once the hindrance is revealed, ask Jesus to speak or show you the truth you need to remove whatever is in the way. You may need to repeat this process multiple times, as each new question or exploration with the Lord may reveal new lie beliefs that are hidden in our hearts, but that greatly influence our choices. Some lie beliefs come from experiences that have left wounds or hurts in our hearts. If that is the case for you, ask Jesus to take you back to the memory where you first "learned" the lie belief that caused your wound. Once you are in your memory and connected to the feeling of the memory, ask Jesus to show you where He is in the memory. Finally, ask Him to speak truth into your heart to replace the lie you believe. Lie beliefs can include lies about yourself, such as "I don't matter," "I am bad," "I am worthless, unimportant, unloved" etc.; lies based on fear, such as "I am out of control," "I must be in control," "I have to," and "I can't," and the last two beliefs in connection with each other; and, lies based on shame, such as "I am bad" and "it is all my fault," or the projection of that belief onto others that it is someone else's fault.

If you continue to struggle to get past the distractions, obstacles, and wounds that may be hindering your conversation with Jesus, ask someone you trust who you know loves the Lord to sit with you and pray with you. You do not necessarily need or want them to pray aloud, but as you converse in your heart with the Lord, ask them to silently pray against the interference of the enemy, and to ask Jesus to reveal Himself to you. He may speak to them to reveal hindrances that you are too blocked to see, and this may aid in knowing what to pursue with Jesus in your prayer. However, they cannot hear the truth for you, any more than someone else knowing Jesus can result in you knowing Jesus. You must know Him through your own experience of Him, and you must receive His truth directly from Him in your heart.

Because of Christ's completed work on the cross, we have been given the opportunity to experience the intimacy with Him that both He and we desire. So, I encourage you, without making it ritual or following any kind of programming, to settle into your heart, quiet your mind in the ways that work best for you, and then simply sit in silence and solitude and have a conversation as you would with a dear friend.

An important concept to keep in mind is that Jesus desires to have an intimate, connected, meaningful, real, present, and deep relationship with you, even more than you do with Him. He is your partner and your best friend. If you seek His presence, He will help you to experience Him, and to develop that type of ongoing connection where you can ask Him anything, talk to Him about everything, and feel Him with you in all things.

And so I leave you with the question that Jesus posed to Peter: Who do you say Jesus is?

Notes

Final Thoughts

For Additional Study

Made in the USA
Lexington, KY
26 February 2017